# Eastern England Verses
Edited by Mark Richardson

First published in Great Britain in 2007 by:
Young Writers
Remus House
Coltsfoot Drive
Peterborough
PE2 9JX
Telephone: 01733 890066
Website: www.youngwriters.co.uk

All Rights Reserved

© Copyright Contributors 2006

SB ISBN 1 84602 713 6

# Foreword

Young Writers was established in 1991 and has been passionately devoted to the promotion of reading and writing in children and young adults ever since. The quest continues today. Young Writers remains as committed to the nurturing of poetic and literary talent as ever.

This year's Young Writers competition has proven as vibrant and dynamic as ever and we are delighted to present a showcase of the best poetry from across the UK and in some cases overseas. Each poem has been selected from a wealth of *A Pocketful Of Rhyme* entries before ultimately being published in this, our fourteenth primary school poetry series.

Once again, we have been supremely impressed by the overall quality of the entries we have received. The imagination, energy and creativity which has gone into each young writer's entry made choosing the poems a challenging and often difficult but ultimately hugely rewarding task - the general high standard of the work submitted ensured this opportunity to bring their poetry to a larger appreciative audience.

We sincerely hope you are pleased with this final collection and that you will enjoy *A Pocketful Of Rhyme Eastern England Verses* for many years to come.

# Contents

| | |
|---|---|
| Charlie Coles (9) | 1 |
| Lopa Banerjee (10) | 2 |

**Brown's CE Primary School, Sleaford**
| | |
|---|---|
| Tilly Capel (11) | 3 |
| Ben Borrill (10) | 4 |

**Bunny CE Primary School, Nottingham**
| | |
|---|---|
| Matt Hodgkins (8) | 5 |
| Charlie Sprosen (8) | 6 |
| Samuel Wilby (8) | 7 |
| Abigail Lewin (7) | 8 |
| Miles Shirtcliffe (8) | 9 |
| Isabella Srodzinski-Stevens (7) | 10 |

**Canewdon Endowed Primary School, Rochford**
| | |
|---|---|
| Charlotte Holmes (10) | 11 |
| Joshua Bedford (10) | 12 |
| Scarlet Marchant (10) | 13 |
| Lauren Tagg (10) | 14 |
| Olivia Meeson (10) | 15 |
| Tatchiana Deer (10) | 16 |
| Shay Peters (10) | 17 |
| Mitchell Harley (10) | 18 |
| Stevie Bryan (11) | 19 |
| Jordan Millgate (10) | 20 |

**Clare Middle School, Clare**
| | |
|---|---|
| Ashleigh Read (10) | 21 |
| Robert Jackson (10) | 22 |
| Alfie Frost (10) | 23 |
| Chloe Groom (10) | 24 |
| Jessie Baxter (10) | 25 |
| Eleanor Barrett (10) | 26 |
| Rebecca Clarke (10) | 27 |
| Elizabeth Huck (10) | 28 |
| Owen Hender (10) | 29 |
| Lucy Rose (10) | 30 |

| | |
|---|---|
| Harry Beavis (10) | 31 |
| Oliver Clark (10) | 32 |
| Danielle Byford (10) | 33 |
| Molly Moroney (10) | 34 |
| Emilie Wilkins (10) | 35 |
| Cameron Floyd (10) | 36 |
| Joy Steed (10) | 37 |
| Molly Murlis (10) | 38 |
| Kirsty Habel (10) | 39 |
| Chelsea Hardy (11) | 40 |

**Edward Worlledge Middle School, Great Yarmouth**

| | |
|---|---|
| Casey-Jo Williams (8) | 41 |
| Heather Wells (8) | 42 |
| Kyle Manning (9) | 43 |
| Dale Jermy (8) | 44 |
| Goncalo de Castro (8) | 45 |
| Abbie Plumber (8) | 46 |
| Jack Harvey (8) | 47 |
| Ina De Almeida (8) | 48 |
| Hadley Hughes (8) | 49 |
| Daniel Kennedy (8) | 50 |
| Rhianna Phipps (8) | 51 |
| Harry Carter (8) | 52 |
| Nikita Berry (8) | 53 |
| Tabitha Borgenvik (8) | 54 |
| Dalton Stamp (8) | 55 |
| Demi Cumby (8) | 56 |
| Daniel Chapman (8) | 57 |
| Erin Horne (9) | 58 |

**Lynncroft Primary School, Nottingham**

| | |
|---|---|
| Wesleigh Lawson (11) | 59 |
| Lauren Quinn (10) | 60 |
| Tom Annable (10) | 61 |
| Harley-Jay Harris (10) | 62 |
| Kyle Connolly (10) | 63 |
| Oliver George (11) | 64 |
| Cullen Canlin (10) | 65 |
| Bethany Watson (10) | 66 |
| Jessica Bates (10) | 67 |

| | |
|---|---|
| Rebecca Elston (10) | 68 |
| Kieran Paull (10) | 69 |
| Paige Roadley (10) | 70 |
| Adam Clements (11) | 71 |
| Callum Rowland (10) | 72 |
| Emma Rowe (10) | 73 |
| Liam Bamford (10) | 74 |
| Tamzin Wood (10) | 75 |
| Ellis Pullen (10) | 76 |
| Chrissie Morris (10) | 77 |
| George Wadsley (10) | 78 |
| Maisie Clifton (10) | 79 |
| Abigail Coward (10) | 80 |
| Shanice Stewart (11) | 81 |
| Sally Shipley (10) | 82 |

**Maylandsea Community Primary School, Chelmsford**

| | |
|---|---|
| Jack Jeffreys (9) | 83 |
| Bobby Carabine (9) | 84 |
| Andrew Boden (9) | 85 |
| James Thame (9) | 86 |
| Josh Oxley (9) | 87 |
| Charlotte Hayman (9) | 88 |
| Maisie-Jane Emans (9) | 89 |
| Ellie Hazell (9) | 90 |
| Ashleigh Paul (9) | 91 |
| Samantha Neill (9) | 92 |
| Francesca Moore (9) | 93 |
| Luke Brightly (10) | 94 |
| Joseph Thorpe (9) | 95 |
| Christopher Windows (9) | 96 |
| Ben Braden (9) | 97 |
| Joe Walker (9) | 98 |
| Hayley Anderson (9) | 99 |
| Abbie McGovern (9) | 100 |
| Jay Craske (9) | 101 |
| Samuel Lowman (9) | 102 |
| Tom Pearce (9) | 103 |
| Joe Willis (9) | 104 |
| Zoe Watling (9) | 105 |
| Harvey Acton (9) | 106 |

| | |
|---|---|
| Matthew Foulser  (9) | 107 |
| Pierce Newton  (10) | 108 |
| Tyler Robinson  (9) | 109 |
| Megan Plumb  (9) | 110 |
| Ellie Godley  (9) | 111 |

## Morton CE Primary School, Bourne

| | |
|---|---|
| Talia Karim  (10) | 112 |
| Ryan Compton  (9) | 113 |
| Edward Mumby  (10) | 114 |
| Renee Dams  (9) | 115 |
| Georgia Thirtle  (9) | 116 |
| Lewis Pressley  (11) | 117 |
| Jack Smith  (10) | 118 |
| Alastair Pope  (10) | 119 |
| Hannah Thompson  (9) | 120 |
| Kayleigh Lambe  (9) | 121 |
| Shannon McPherson  (10) | 122 |
| Jack Graham  (10) | 123 |
| Craig Turner  (10) | 124 |
| Ashley Dacre  (10) | 125 |
| Liam Davidson  (10) | 126 |
| Talys Andres  (9) | 127 |
| Davin Phenix (10) | 128 |
| Felicity Mitchell (9) | 129 |
| Jennifer McAndrew  (9) | 130 |
| Georgina Wilkie  (10) | 131 |
| Eleanor Davies  (10) | 132 |
| Callum Lusty  (11) | 133 |
| Samuel Doe  (10) | 134 |
| James Thomas  (10) | 135 |
| Michael Montgomery  (9) | 136 |

## Rampton Primary, Retford

| | |
|---|---|
| Megan Slinger  (9) | 137 |
| James Lofthouse  (10) | 138 |
| Scarlett Cordall  (9) | 139 |
| Hayden Birkett  (9) | 140 |
| Josh Gillott  (11) & Jack Eddy  (10) | 141 |
| Carter Marson  (9) | 142 |
| Lucy Presley  (9) | 143 |

**St Peter's Primary School, Colchester**
Nicholas Kemp (10)     144
George Styles (10)     145
Oliver Dean (10)     146
Thomas Randerson (10)     147
Angus Unsworth (11)     148
Luke Norman (10)     149
William Mills (11)     150
Charlotte Self (10)     151
Joshua Forbes-Brown (10)     152
Aaron Osborne (10)     153
Jack O'Byrne (10)     154

**Thanet Primary School, Hull**
Ellie Newton (9)     155
Sophie-Claire Webster (9)     156
Jade Wiles (9)     157

**Waddington Redwood Primary School, Lincoln**
Luke Eeles (10)     158
Molly Barker (9)     159
John Melligan (10)     160
Lewis Anthony (9)     161
Caitlin Barker (10)     162
Lauren Burnley (10)     163
Charlotte Flint (10)     164
Hayley Flint (10)     165
Gezamin Parry     166
Carys Thomas     167
James Ekins     168
Emily Pavier (10)     169
Sara Edwards     170
Jay Bellis (9)     171
Aimee Hayward (10)     172
Jack Woolsey (10)     173
Kelly Warren (10)     174
Robbie Green (10)     175
Jake Rigby (10)     176

*with love from*

Joshua

xxx

## The Poems

# Emotions

Why am I feeling so low?
Sad and depressed and grey,
This horrible day is not going away.

Why am I feeling so happy?
Not sad in any way
I'm having a cheerful day!

**Charlie Coles (9)**

## Seasonings

Cinnamon and salt,
Paprika, pepper and vinegar malt,
Our good seasonings five,
Are also important to keep tasty food alive.

With these five on exquisite food,
There is absolutely no reason to brood,
If thou would go into thy vault,
Be sure to check your supply of salt.

Now you have learnt,
That, if your food is burnt,
Remember paprika, pepper, cinnamon, salt,
(Do not forget vinegar malt),
Seasonings will save the day!

**Lopa Banerjee (10)**

# Silly Tilly

There was a young girl called Tilly,
Whose answers were sometimes quite silly,
Asked before told,
'What country is cold?'
And poor silly Tilly said, 'Chile.'

The teacher sent her home straight away,
And was told to come back the next day,
She explained to her mum,
Who thought she was rum,
But said, 'You're my daughter so, hey!'

She went back to school the next week,
The teacher then gave a loud shriek
For Tilly was right,
And so she was bright,
So Miss made her brain of the week!

**Tilly Capel (11)**
**Brown's CE Primary School, Sleaford**

# Henry VIII

We all remember Henry
A king in Tudor times.
To know much more about him
Just read this Tudor rhyme.

Our good old King Henry,
Is he heavy, fat or thin?
Is he very kind or cruel?
Is he a brilliant King?

Our good old King Henry
Does a lot of sport,
He plays a lot of tennis
When his wife's in court.

Our good old King Henry
Got married to six wives.
He had three different children,
Two girls, one boy who died.

The first she was named Mary,
The second Elizabeth.
The boy was called Edward,
At fifteen was his death.

Our good old King Henry
Likes a mammoth feast.
Chicken, pig and wine,
He eats just like a beast.

Our good old King Henry,
The church he tried to bin,
So he could divorce his wife
And marry Anne Boleyn.

That's our good King Henry, I hope you've learned a bit,
Believe me you want to meet him, he's rather quite a wit.

**Ben Borrill (10)**
Brown's CE Primary School, Sleaford

## Cricket Is Cruel

Cricket is cruel
You get hit with a ball!
You look at the score
And sit on the floor
Because you know
You're not gonna win
You throw your hopes in the bin!
Until you win!
You scream and shout
And dance about.
Have a bath
Drink de-caff
But you have been smacked
In the face
By the bat
Ha ha!

**Matt Hodgkins (8)**
**Bunny CE Primary School, Nottingham**

## The River Alone

I'm always wet.
I'm always see-through.
I see the boats rush by.
The wind blows to make my waves
And the blue colour of the sky.
Night will fall.
My colour turns to black.
I'm all alone in the dark black sky
Na night.

**Charlie Sprosen (8)**
**Bunny CE Primary School, Nottingham**

# Castle

Us two are very very tall and very very cold.
When the ovens are on I get quite hot.
But when sun falls all you can hear are the loud sounds of snoring
in here.
When it's morning they ring big bells
Which make a big sound to wake everyone up.
When visitors come we open the gates to let them in
But when bad guys come, we shut the gates and kick them out.
In the moat there are huge sharks in our big moat.
Near the bottom it is very very dark and gloomy
That's where all the human bones are, right at the bottom of our
big moat,
And all about our big castle.

**Samuel Wilby (8)**
**Bunny CE Primary School, Nottingham**

# Friends

Friends, friends how I like friends.
I like them so much I love them so much
I go to their house, oh how I love friends.
Friends are everywhere
But friends are sometimes naughty,
So friends, friends go away and I feel lonely,
Very, very lonely.
Friends, my favourite things,
Friends, friends, friends, friends,
I love them.

**Abigail Lewin (7)**
**Bunny CE Primary School, Nottingham**

# River

A river is a wet place.
A river is where we swim.
A secret spot to have a chat.
A perfect place to make a den.
A nice place to sit in the sun.
A secret place to find a house.
A place to hide and watch the birds.

**Miles Shirtcliffe (8)**
**Bunny CE Primary School, Nottingham**

# Friends

Friends, friends
I do like
They are fun
They are kind
You can go to their house
Whenever you like
Friends, friends
I do like.
You can go and sleep at their house
Whenever you like
Goodnight!

**Isabella Srodzinski-Stevens (7)**
Bunny CE Primary School, Nottingham

## Sports

Football, netball what's it gonna be
Baseball, basketball, I need a cup of tea
What one, which one, I don't know what to pick,
Please just give me a great big stick.

**Charlotte Holmes (10)**
**Canewdon Endowed Primary School, Rochford**

# The Golden Sunset

The golden sunset,
Setting in the orange, cloudy sky.
Bringing light to the world,
Saying a cool goodbye.
Never saying anything,
But gives impact to the sky.
As the moon rises,
It brings light to the big black sky.
Once again it disappears,
And now the moon is high.
Now the sun rises,
And brings light to the poor.
The big moon has gone now,
And the sun shines once more.

**Joshua Bedford (10)**
**Canewdon Endowed Primary School, Rochford**

# Horses

I love horses, yes I do
I love horses, they're so cute
I love horses yes I do
I love horses they're so pretty
Because they're the best friends you can ever have.

**Scarlet Marchant (10)**
Canewdon Endowed Primary School, Rochford

## What's A Best Friend?

Someone who you can trust to always be there for you,
To pick you up and make you feel ten times better!

Someone you can play with and eat your dinner next to,
You tell a joke and have a laugh,
And then say, 'See you tomorrow!'

**Lauren Tagg (10)**
Canewdon Endowed Primary School, Rochford

## The Pixie

In a village far, far away,
There is a pixie, sleeping day by day,
But there is a problem, when he wakes up,
He is very thirsty, he wants his golden cup,
At midnight he gets his wooden fiddle,
And lures children's dreams with his sparkling riddle,
Into his golden cup they go,
With a colourful, wonderful, musical flow,
So after this he is thirsty no more,
He goes to sleep, and shuts the door.

**Olivia Meeson (10)**
**Canewdon Endowed Primary School, Rochford**

# My Poem

Dancing on logs,
Crawling up trees,
Shooting up flowers,
Stings even the bees.
Singing its lament,
Dancing along,
Animals perish,
In hearing its song.
A glimmering glow,
Of yellow and red,
A flower it looks like,
But can behead.
Man's friend and man's enemy,
Saves lives and takes them too,
And if you're not careful,
It'll take the life of you.
A beautiful creature,
And terrible too,
Afraid of water,
But not of you.
A deadly weapon,
A terrible shame,
A horrible monster,
But not really to blame.
Defeating the darkness,
The coldness and gloom,
For this deadly flower,
Is now in full bloom.

These are all clues,
What is it?

**Tatchiana Deer (10)**
**Canewdon Endowed Primary School, Rochford**

# Football

F ootball is fun
O h, football, come
O n the pitch
T alking about football
B all on the floor
A ll on the tour
L ove football
L ove to play football.

**Shay Peters (10)**
**Canewdon Endowed Primary School, Rochford**

## My Pet

My pet is small, my pet is fat,
My pet has a mouth but my pet can't chat.
That's because my pet's a cat.

**Mitchell Harley (10)**
Canewdon Endowed Primary School, Rochford

# Family Poem

My mum's the sort of person
Who's never grumpy.

My dad's the sort of person
Who never cheers up.

My brother's the sort of person
Who never gives up.

My sister's the sort of person
Who you wouldn't want to mess with

And I'm the person who sums it all up.

**Stevie Bryan (11)**
**Canewdon Endowed Primary School, Rochford**

## Manchester

M anchester is so cool
A wicked place
N ame is Manchester
C an't beat them
H ates scousers
E verybody loves them
S houts 'We are the best.'
T he best team
E ats the other teams
R ed devils.

**Jordan Millgate (10)**
Canewdon Endowed Primary School, Rochford

## Midnight Dancing Stars

When I fall asleep,
I always snore very deep,
I get a big fright,
Because the clock strikes midnight,
When I look out of the window,
I see the sparkling midnight stars flow,
They start sparkling and dancing in the midnight glow,
I sit there watching them in the night sky,
I see how they are so up high,
I love to watch the sparkling stars,
When I hear the noisy cars,
I know it is morning and go to sleep,
Then again I still snore deep,
When I wake up I see the sun,
Then I think back because I have had so much
Fun!

**Ashleigh Read (10)**
Clare Middle School, Clare

## I Wish I Were A Wall

I wish I were a wall
Who was really tall
I could see around
Be above the ground
And the people are
*Small!*

**Robert Jackson (10)**
**Clare Middle School, Clare**

## I Wish I Could Be A Football

I wish I could be a football
And score lots of goals.
Be internationally famous and
Please a million souls.
Earn a lot of money.
Now I'm waiting for the shot.
Ronaldo in his flashy boots
Smashing me in the net.
One - nil United
What a fabulous goal!
Yes! That's the final whistle
Now it's been blown!

**Alfie Frost (10)**
Clare Middle School, Clare

## I Wish I Were

I wish I were a carpet,
I would lie around all day,
I wish I were a bubble,
I would fly about and play,

I wish I were a teddy bear,
Children would cuddle me,
I wish I were a fish,
I would be as happy as could be,

I don't know what I want to be,
Or should I just be me,
Please help me, please help me,
I don't know what to be.

**Chloe Groom (10)**
Clare Middle School, Clare

# Fish

There once was a fish sailing through the water,
A man threw in some money,
And he hit his head on the quarter,
So he jumped up and said,
'Hey you, you hit me on the head.'
The man turned round and was amazed to see no one there.

**Jessie Baxter (10)**
Clare Middle School, Clare

## Howie The Horse!

There was a horse called Howie,
He loves to play basketball!

When his owners are out,
He goes out onto the pitch and plays!

He plays with his favourite ball,
Which is blue and brown.

But when his owners are in,
He is still happy!

**Eleanor Barrett (10)**
**Clare Middle School, Clare**

## Polly The Pony

Sitting in her stable,
Like a baby in a cradle,
Polly the pony wanted to go out and about,
So she pulled on her coat,
And out she went down past the town,
She started to get tired.
Like a pride of lions after they've eaten.
So back she went home, home, home,
To her stable,
Where she fell asleep, fast asleep.

**Rebecca Clarke (10)**
**Clare Middle School, Clare**

## My Tapping Shoes

As I tie the lace, a beaming smile comes from my feet.
Each toe a tap a
      Tap
            Tap as my shoes tap away and carry me
With them.
    Indents and files mark their smiles, my toes are beaming now.
If I dance anymore I will be a pile of bones and muscle on the floor.
My shoes of silk drink lots of milk to keep them nice and strong,
They also drink milk to keep them going on.

**Elizabeth Huck (10)**
**Clare Middle School, Clare**

## The Dragon Of Doom

The dragon is in his lair,
Sleeping on his gold,
He is happy crunching on human bones,
Or fighting for wealthy thrones.

**Owen Hender (10)**
**Clare Middle School, Clare**

## My Marvellous Mouse

My marvellous mouse has his own little house,
And his family all speak Spanish.
He does magic tricks to make me vanish.
All my friends think he's cute,
But sometimes he turns me into a newt.
Then my mum throws me out the house,
Whilst shouting, 'First feed your mouse!'

**Lucy Rose (10)**
**Clare Middle School, Clare**

## The Shark

I wish I was a shark
With shiny white teeth

I bit a man on a surfboard
He chased me
He was a fraud.

He threw a sword
It went straight through me
I dropped
I dropped
I hit the floor
And flopped.

I had a good funeral
But it ended in tears
But with God I had a few cheers!

**Harry Beavis (10)**
**Clare Middle School, Clare**

## The House

There was a monster house,
A child was cycling along,
She rode past the house,
Suddenly the house turned to life,
The door opened, the mat flung out.

The windows turned to eyes,
The roof tiles turned to hair,
The man next door heard a scream,
He goes outside but nothing,
The house was exactly the same.

**Oliver Clark (10)**
Clare Middle School, Clare

## My Guinea Pig

My guinea pig,
Went to a birthday gig,
Went on the X-Factor,
Got a job as an actor,
Got the sack,
Brought a rucksack,
And went and sat,
On my doormat.

**Danielle Byford (10)**
**Clare Middle School, Clare**

## My Wobbly Tooth

My wobbly tooth,
Is shouting at me,
'Let me out, take me out
I really don't care
As long as I am out.
I want to explore every day.'
I said to him, 'You'll have to pay,'
So now he wants to stay.
I woke up in the morning,
My tooth is still snoring,
I pulled it out, it gave a shout,
Now it's well and truly out!

**Molly Moroney (10)**
Clare Middle School, Clare

## My Ant

Even though they may be small,
The ant has a mouth that's big and tall.

I took him to the show one day,
And lost him in a pile of hay.

I hope he hasn't forgotten his map,
He's probably had a little nap.

Then I heard a little noise,
It was my little anty's voice.

And soon I found him,
He was next to the bin.

It's lucky he is loud,
Or he wouldn't have been found.

Even though his mouth that's big and tall,
It's useful when he needs to call!

**Emilie Wilkins (10)**
**Clare Middle School, Clare**

## My Headlice

As the children scurry around,
The adult lice,
Have a lie in,
They chit and chat most of the morning,
Until the phone rings,
Bling, bling.

**Cameron Floyd (10)**
**Clare Middle School, Clare**

## In The Park

In the park leaves rustle,
As the trees try to talk.
Plants and flowers sway;
As the wind
Blows on them gently.

**Joy Steed (10)**
**Clare Middle School, Clare**

## I Wish I Were A Hairbrush

I wish I were a hairbrush
Brushing away and away.

I would love to feel all the smooth hair,
And to make all the knots go away.

I would love to be a hairbrush,
Brushing through all the family's hair,
Whether it is long hair,
Short hair, light hair or dark hair.

I would love to be a hairbrush,
Brushing away and away.

**Molly Murlis (10)**
Clare Middle School, Clare

## My Two Front Teeth

My two front teeth
Are big and *bold*
They always cuddle
When they're cold
They go to sleep
When they are told
They wake me up
When they are old.
When they play they
Wobble to the sound
And beat when I chew.
They'll soon be gone,
Fallen out,
Gone to the Tooth Fairy
In her pouch.

**Kirsty Habel (10)**
**Clare Middle School, Clare**

## The Chair That Breathes Fire

There was a chair who was fed up
He was fed up for lots of reasons but these particular things
Made him very cross:
Thing 1: he hated being sat on.
Thing 2: all the other chairs laughed at him because he was small.
Well now he was going to pay them back he plucked up his courage
And . . . *boom* the fire from the middle of his mouth burnt them all
And they were all burnt to a crisp.
No one bothered him again.

**Chelsea Hardy (11)**
**Clare Middle School, Clare**

# Love

Love is when you go really pink like fresh new roses.
Love sounds like birds singing to you very sweetly.
Love tastes like a pile of strawberries ready to eat.
Love looks like bunnies, so happy hugging each other.
Love feels like you're in fairy world with lots of fairies and The
                                        Wizard of Oz.
Love reminds you that everybody respects you and cares for you.

**Casey-Jo Williams (8)**
**Edward Worlledge Middle School, Great Yarmouth**

## Ruby-Red

Ruby-red is the colour of love.
It brings a soft touch to me and you.
Can you feel the love?
It feels like a new start again.
The sounds of the little birds singing songs.
Love looks like red roses everywhere.
Love reminds me of flowers and babies being born.

**Heather Wells (8)**
**Edward Worlledge Middle School, Great Yarmouth**

# Anger

Anger is like a bubbly, volcano,
Anger tastes like a hot chilli pepper.
Anger looks like a fire burning in a fireplace.
Anger sounds like a crackling fireball.
Anger feels like being hit with a bucket of hot water.
Anger looks like the colours of a dolphin black and grey.

**Kyle Manning (9)**
**Edward Worlledge Middle School, Great Yarmouth**

## Love

The colour of love is like a pink nose of a rabbit.
Love sounds like sweetness in a field all day long.
Love tastes like cherryade crackly and bubbly.
Love looks cuddly, loving and caring.
Love feels like squashing in-between your toenails.
Love reminds you of kisses.

**Dale Jermy (8)**
**Edward Worlledge Middle School, Great Yarmouth**

## Scared

The colour of scared is black and dark green like you know who.
It looks like nothing whatsoever.
It feels like nothing forever
And it reminds you of a car crash and a bear and snakes
attacking you.

It tastes like a dog that has been,
And it sounds like loud screams.

**Goncalo de Castro (8)**
**Edward Worlledge Middle School, Great Yarmouth**

## Anger

Anger is the colour of bright fiery blood.
Anger feels like a hot volcano ready to explode.
Anger tastes like a burning drink in my mouth.
Anger sounds like a massive earthquake.
Anger looks like a roaring lion catching his prey.
Anger reminds me of a booming headache.

**Abbie Plumber (8)**
**Edward Worlledge Middle School, Great Yarmouth**

## Love

Love is pink like bubbles in a bath.
Love sounds like waves splashing up onto a rock.
Love tastes like strawberries squirting juice into my mouth.
Love looks like angels' wings.
Love feels like babies' skin.
Love reminds me of being born.

**Jack Harvey (8)**
**Edward Worlledge Middle School, Great Yarmouth**

## Happiness

Happiness is like bright yellow sunflowers laying on the grass.
Happiness sounds like a baby's laughter.
Happiness tastes like a sweet, creamy chocolate ice cream
With strawberry syrup on top.
Happiness feels like you're in Heaven.
Happiness looks like you're the luckiest person in the world.
Happiness reminds me of my grandma.

**Ina De Almeida (8)**
**Edward Worlledge Middle School, Great Yarmouth**

# Happy

When you're happy your face appears yellow.
When you're happy your mouth is cheerful.
It tastes like corn on the cob.
It looks like someone's happy.
It feels like flowers growing.
It reminds you of happiness.

**Hadley Hughes (8)**
**Edward Worlledge Middle School, Great Yarmouth**

## Darkness

Darkness is like a black and grey twirling hole.
It sounds like drums, your heart is beating very loud in a weird
rhythm.
Darkness tastes like poison and blood dripping into your mouth.
It looks like a black corner with silky cobwebs and eight-legged
spiders.
It feels like you are being sucked down into a deep black hole.
It reminds you of a shadow monster creeping around
When you are sleeping in the darkness.

**Daniel Kennedy (8)**
**Edward Worlledge Middle School, Great Yarmouth**

# Love

Love is like beautiful yellow and pink roses in the garden.
Love sounds like beautiful birds singing in the treetops.
Love tastes like gorgeous cherries from a blossom tree.
Love looks like two bunny rabbits in the air, kissing.
Love feels like flying through the sky.
Love reminds me of the world just beginning.

**Rhianna Phipps (8)**
**Edward Worlledge Middle School, Great Yarmouth**

## Sad

Sadness is red like a flame.
Sadness sounds like someone crying.
Sadness tastes like a squashed banana.
Sadness looks like a deadly stare.
Sadness feels like someone's hitting you.
Sadness reminds me of a child crying.

**Harry Carter (8)**
**Edward Worlledge Middle School, Great Yarmouth**

## Love

Love is pink like a beautiful princess in her ballgown.
Love sounds like beating hearts.
Love tastes like strawberry juice in my mouth.
Love feels like candyfloss and clouds.
Love reminds you of hugging a teddy that feels all squishy.

**Nikita Berry (8)**
**Edward Worlledge Middle School, Great Yarmouth**

## Laughter

Laughter is bright red, like a bright and shiny light.
Laughter sounds like the whole world giggling like a bunch of monkeys.
Laughter looks like a greedy doggy dancing and being silly.
Laughter feels like a massage chair moving around the room.
Laughter reminds you of the funny days you have had.

**Tabitha Borgenvik (8)**
**Edward Worlledge Middle School, Great Yarmouth**

# Anger

Anger is like a red flaming fire.
Anger sounds like a fierce, growling tiger.
Anger tastes like a hot chilli pepper.
Anger looks like a fiery flaming beast.
Anger feels like a hot steaming bath.
Anger reminds me of children smashing windows.

**Dalton Stamp (8)**
**Edward Worlledge Middle School, Great Yarmouth**

# Love

Love is sweet pink like rose petals twirling through the air.
Love sounds like a gentle lullaby being sung softly to a sleeping child.
Love tastes like candyfloss melting on my tongue.
Love looks like a angel sitting on a comfy flower case.
Love feels like pink and purple hearts bursting out of my belly.
Love reminds me of a baby girl in her cot.

**Demi Cumby (8)**
**Edward Worlledge Middle School, Great Yarmouth**

## Happy

Happiness is yellow like a shining sun.
Happiness is like a really fast heartbeat.
Happiness tastes like smooth, melting chocolate.
Happiness looks like a really big smile.
Happiness feels like huge bubbles in the air.
Happiness reminds me of my nanny's dog called Patch.

**Daniel Chapman (8)**
**Edward Worlledge Middle School, Great Yarmouth**

## Laughter

Laughter is orange like sweet juice from a nectarine.
Laughter sounds like birds tweeting with the sound of joy.
Laughter tastes like hot chocolate, freshly made.
Laughter looks like pretty butterflies flying from flower to flower.
Laughter feels like a buzzy bee landing on my nose.
Laughter reminds me of boys and girls having fun.

**Erin Horne (9)**
**Edward Worlledge Middle School, Great Yarmouth**

## Terror

I scream
The island was being swallowed behind me,
It took my house and everything in it.
The volcano erupted.
The sky was lava,
A wave of fire snapped the bridge
I ran, I ran for my life.
I stumbled and tripped.
I saw my whole life before me.
Then a tsunami of water hurled me.
I rested at the bottom of the ocean.

**Wesleigh Lawson (11)**
Lynncroft Primary School, Nottingham

## Dark Night
Silence is black like the dark, dark night.
The owls are hooting and the blackbird sleeping.
The wind was blowing outside.
The cat was making no noise in a dark night.

**Lauren Quinn (10)**
**Lynncroft Primary School, Nottingham**

## Love

Love is red like a bunch of rich red roses.
I love my mum, dad, and my cat.
My mum gives me cuddles.
My dad takes me out.
My cat loves me because he rubs my leg.
I love them all.

**Tom Annable (10)**
**Lynncroft Primary School, Nottingham**

## Silent Snow

Silence is like white snow falling from the sky.
It tastes like water.
I like it when it is quiet.
It is peaceful.
Soon the snow will melt.

**Harley-Jay Harris (10)**
**Lynncroft Primary School, Nottingham**

## Sad To Happy

Sadness is blue
Like the deep blue sea.
I don't want to be sad
I want to be happy.
My friends come to play
I'm not sad
We have a fun day.

**Kyle Connolly (10)**
**Lynncroft Primary School, Nottingham**

## The Scream

The sky was being overpowered by fresh lava from
                              an erupting volcano.
My house!
My island!
My *life!*
It's all gone, gone, *gone!*
It was raining blood with millions of fireballs being pelted.
Faster than the speed of light.
It's a tragedy!
Everything it touched turned to ash.
Everyone I know has been demolished!
*Next, me!*

**Oliver George (11)**
**Lynncroft Primary School, Nottingham**

## The Scream

He stands head in hands,
Screaming for his life.
Sky as red as lava,
Engulfing him,
Water overflows,
Faster, faster it comes,
Will he survive?

**Cullen Canlin (10)**
**Lynncroft Primary School, Nottingham**

## Dying Inside

As the volcano erupted in the sky
I screeched
The sky was as red as the blood in your body
The boat went out to sea
The water was bashing the boat
I fell
It was horrible
Then behind me there was a man
I knew my life was over
I felt like I was dying inside.

**Bethany Watson (10)**
**Lynncroft Primary School, Nottingham**

## The Last Breath

The sky is a burning wave of lava
Coming to swallow my island,
With me on it.
Air smells of ash
That will cover and destroy my culture.
I scream, I shout.
Heat engulfs me
Then silence
All I can see is darkness
Suddenly I have gone.

**Jessica Bates (10)**
**Lynncroft Primary School, Nottingham**

## The Scream

The sea, like fire, blue to red.
The sky of blood is falling.
I'm melting, melting into nothing.
A scream.
I awake from this horrible nightmare.
Afraid of this nasty dream coming true.
I dream no more of rainbows and flowers,
But of death and depression.

**Rebecca Elston (10)**
**Lynncroft Primary School, Nottingham**

# Apocalypse

The air turns to ash,
I scream,
The Earth is coming to an end.
The Heaven's open,
The ash sinks into my skin,
It is time,
I lie on the floor,
Rest in peace.

**Kieran Paull (10)**
**Lynncroft Primary School, Nottingham**

## The Dark, Dark Night

The erupting burnt sky is as red as a pool of fresh blood.
I turn back, I scream.
My island, my home, gone forever.
I shiver at the thought of me being next.
I am right.
Death has found me . . .

**Paige Roadley (10)**
**Lynncroft Primary School, Nottingham**

## Death In The World

The beach - sinking like hot lava raining down from the sky.
The bridge - collapsing while the blasting whirlpool pulls the dark
island under.
The sky - hot lava pouring down, melting the world to an early end.
The screams - deafening like an earthquake and the world floats
Into outer space.

**Adam Clements (11)**
**Lynncroft Primary School, Nottingham**

# The Scream

The sky - as red as lava
Raining lava
Would everyone melt?
Help us
The heat, burning my soul,
Melting the earth around me.
Death surrounds me
I fall,
Screaming,
Disaster!

**Callum Rowland (10)**
**Lynncroft Primary School, Nottingham**

## Scream

Blood-red sky
As an erupting volcano.
I am horrified.
The island behind me is melting away.
All those people dying.
I'm lucky I'm still alive.
I can hear screaming in the horizon.
Screaming of homeless folk with no place to live.
I would soon become one of them.

**Emma Rowe (10)**
**Lynncroft Primary School, Nottingham**

## Scream

The sky - is as red as blood and lava.
The sea - curves through the island
Like a snake charging towards me, to swallow me.
The posts behind me - remind me of my worst nightmare.
The bridge - crack, 'Argh' foot's trapped.
The waves - they're too high, I'm going to drown.

**Liam Bamford (10)**
Lynncroft Primary School, Nottingham

# The Darkness

The sky looks like blood,
It's raining eyeballs.
My hair has gone.
A wall of water splashed me.
My boats are sinking.
The water is red and black.
My foot is stuck.
Oh no I think there is someone behind me.
I welcome the darkness.

**Tamzin Wood (10)**
**Lynncroft Primary School, Nottingham**

## The Scream

The sky opening
Releasing my worst nightmare
Land depositing water taking over
The red sky running fire
I can see my body melting
Into the water
My death is coming.

**Ellis Pullen (10)**
**Lynncroft Primary School, Nottingham**

## Danger To Death

The sky has never looked so red,
As red as lava,
Raining blood,
The dark blue sea,
Floats under me and starts to defeat,
I see my island
Sinking in the dark blue sea
I scream.

**Chrissie Morris (10)**
**Lynncroft Primary School, Nottingham**

## The Screams

The big black boat was pouring in with blood,
Sinking, slowly, slowly,
I could hear big roars of screams,
Loads of people falling off, into the blood,
The sun disappeared into the sky.

**George Wadsley (10)**
**Lynncroft Primary School, Nottingham**

## One Life!

The sky faded quickly,
It started to turn mixes of red, orange and yellow.
The sky caved in on me.
The water swallowed me whole
Like a hissing and spitting rattlesnake.
My life was at risk.
Will I ever wake up from this horrible nightmare?

**Maisie Clifton (10)**
**Lynncroft Primary School, Nottingham**

## The Dark Night

The sea is turning as red as lava
Swirling round and round
Dragging us
Down, down, down.
Thrashing water is coming
To gobble me down in one go
I scream.
But no one can hear my screeching voice.
Here is the end.
The Devil has found me.

**Abigail Coward (10)**
**Lynncroft Primary School, Nottingham**

## Bang! Bang!

*Bang! Bang!*
What's that banging my head?
Against a stone brick wall
With pain and anger
Like a rubber bouncy ball.

**Shanice Stewart (11)**
**Lynncroft Primary School, Nottingham**

## Scream

The sea clashing through the pier
On top of the ledge.
I snap - as if a million knives are stabbing me.

I cling onto the pier
I can feel people's confused faces
The pain!
I scream.
I close my eyes.
I am home.
It was a nightmare.
Just a horrible nightmare.

**Sally Shipley (10)**
**Lynncroft Primary School, Nottingham**

## Happiness

Happiness is multicoloured like a rainbow.
It tastes like Minstrels and Maltesers melted together.
It smells like fresh diesel.
It looks like a rainbow.
It feels like a soft furry cat.
It sounds like a cat purring.

**Jack Jeffreys (9)**
**Maylandsea Community Primary School, Chelmsford**

## Sadness

Sadness is blue, the colour of tears
It tastes like rotten peas
It smells like pumpkins
It looks like people at a funeral
It sounds like a person crying
It feels like water.

**Bobby Carabine (9)**
Maylandsea Community Primary School, Chelmsford

## Grumpiness

Grumpiness is grey like a dull winter's morning,
It tastes like potatoes and avocados on a boring school day,
It smells like manure when you go to a farm,
It looks like Grandpa asleep in his chair, snoring,
It sounds like screaming and shouting right in your ear,
It feels like bird poop dropping on your head!

**Andrew Boden (9)**
**Maylandsea Community Primary School, Chelmsford**

# Fear

Fear is black
Fear tastes like a worm
Fear does smell like an elephant house
Fear does look like pitch-black
Fear does sound like something bad is going to get you
Fear feels like something is breathing on your shoulder.

**James Thame (9)**
Maylandsea Community Primary School, Chelmsford

# Anger

Anger is grey like steam.
It tastes like blood.
It smells like a burnt down house.
It looks like a pack of wolves.
It sounds like a fight.
It feels like a dog biting.

**Josh Oxley (9)**
**Maylandsea Community Primary School, Chelmsford**

# Fear

Fear is a black colour, like a dark cave
It tastes like red-hot spicy chillies
It smells like dead roses
It looks like the aftermath of a bomb exploding
It sounds like a mad, dark, fear monster,
It feels like a big blob, googly monster.

**Charlotte Hayman (9)**
Maylandsea Community Primary School, Chelmsford

# Fear

Fear is the colour black, and it tastes like bitter peas,
It smells like smoke,
It looks like danger,
And it sounds like bombs banging,
And it feels scary and cold.

**Maisie-Jane Emans (9)**
**Maylandsea Community Primary School, Chelmsford**

## Happiness

Happiness is a pink colour
It tastes like a red rose
It smells like chocolate
It looks like a lovely party
It sounds like a quiet day
It feels like a nice, soft rose.

**Ellie Hazell (9)**
**Maylandsea Community Primary School, Chelmsford**

# Fear

Fear is black
It tastes like cold Brussels sprouts
It smells like fields of rotting cabbage
It looks like car crashes on the news
It sounds like shouting and screaming
A feeling like being bullied in the playground,
That's fear.

**Ashleigh Paul (9)**
**Maylandsea Community Primary School, Chelmsford**

## Happiness

Happiness is yellow and orange like the sun.
It tastes like melted chocolate just taken out of the microwave.
It smells like flowers growing in the field.
It looks like animals running around in a field.
It sounds like children laughing.

**Samantha Neill (9)**
**Maylandsea Community Primary School, Chelmsford**

## Happiness

Happiness is yellow like the sun
It tastes like chocolate cakes
It smells sweet
It looks like the sun
It sounds like people giggling
It feels happy.

**Francesca Moore (9)**
**Maylandsea Community Primary School, Chelmsford**

# Happiness

Happiness is bright like the sun.
It tastes like melted chocolate.
It smells like burgers just cooking.
It looks like people running through a field of flowers.
It sounds like a party banging.
It feels like the excitement of getting married.

**Luke Brightly (10)**
Maylandsea Community Primary School, Chelmsford

# Happiness

Happiness tastes like chocolate
Because I like chocolate.

Happiness smells like flowers,
Because they smell like happiness.

It looks like a football pitch.

It sounds like a crowd in a big arena.

It feels like it is your birthday.

**Joseph Thorpe (9)**
**Maylandsea Community Primary School, Chelmsford**

# Fear

Fear is when you're being followed.
It tastes like mouldy Brussels sprouts.
It is red and gloomy and smells like dead people.
Fear is like a person with blood covering his face.
It sounds like footsteps,
And it feels like roaring hot flames.
And it is called Fear.

**Christopher Windows (9)**
**Maylandsea Community Primary School, Chelmsford**

# Anger

Anger is red,
It tastes like sour sweets,
Anger smells like smoke,
It looks like coal burning in a fire,
It sounds like steam coming out of your ears,
It feels like fighting in the playground.

**Ben Braden (9)**
Maylandsea Community Primary School, Chelmsford

## Happiness

It tastes like chocolate
It smells like grass
It looks yellow
It feels good
It sounds like birds.

**Joe Walker (9)**
**Maylandsea Community Primary School, Chelmsford**

# Happiness

Happiness is red like love
It tastes like strawberries
It smells like cherry bubblegum
It looks like balloons popping everywhere
It sounds like party poppers going off
It feels like flower petals soft and smooth.

**Hayley Anderson (9)**
**Maylandsea Community Primary School, Chelmsford**

## Happiness

Happiness is yellow,
Bright like the sun,
It tastes like chocolate,
Melting in my hands,
It smells like flowers,
Swaying in the wind,
It looks like children,
Running in the sun,
It sounds like children,
Screaming in the pool,
It feels like trees,
Dancing in the breeze.

**Abbie McGovern (9)**
Maylandsea Community Primary School, Chelmsford

# Tiredness

Tiredness is black like cake.
It smells like hot chocolate.
It looks like the blackness when you close your eyes.
It sounds like your mum and dad talking in the living room.
It feels like you've done all the things you can do.

**Jay Craske (9)**
**Maylandsea Community Primary School, Chelmsford**

# Happiness

Happiness is yellow like a fresh banana
Happiness tastes like chocolate at a party
Happiness smells like petrol when you spill it
Happiness looks like an overgrown marshmallow
Happiness sounds like a harp from Heaven
Happiness feels like cotton-candy at a funfair.

**Samuel Lowman (9)**
**Maylandsea Community Primary School, Chelmsford**

## Happiness

Happiness is the colour . . . blue!
It tastes like sweet, sweet chocolate
It feels like a ball of fur
It sounds like an owl hooting at me!
But it looks like a picture of me and my friends.

**Tom Pearce (9)**
**Maylandsea Community Primary School, Chelmsford**

## Grumpiness

Grumpiness is grey like an old man's beard,
Grumpiness tastes like mouldy cheese (yuck!)
It smells like seven-year-old bread,
It looks like a short fat man with glasses on a big nose who is 600,
It sounds like a 3-year-old who won't have pasta.
Grumpiness feels like having blood pour out of your ears.

**Joe Willis (9)**
**Maylandsea Community Primary School, Chelmsford**

# Anger

Anger is as grey as a stone
It tastes like rotten eggs
It smells like smoke in a blazing fire
It looks like lightning in the night
It sounds like thunder in the rain
It feels like a very rough rock
After all, I hate anger.

**Zoe Watling (9)**
**Maylandsea Community Primary School, Chelmsford**

# Happiness

Happiness is green as grass
Happiness tastes like mint chocolate
Happiness smells like hot chocolate
Happiness looks like my little brother's bike without stabilisers
Happiness feels soft like a lion's mane.

**Harvey Acton (9)**
**Maylandsea Community Primary School, Chelmsford**

# Happiness

Happiness is the colour red that comes from your smile
Happiness tastes like toffee sweets
Happiness smells like daisies in the sun
Happiness looks like chocolates that are tasty
Happiness sounds like birds that sing
Happiness feels like a smooth black cat.

**Matthew Foulser (9)**
**Maylandsea Community Primary School, Chelmsford**

# Sadness

Sadness is grey, like the writing of a pencil,
It tastes like Brussels sprouts,
It smells like manure in the fields,
It looks like lightning striking in the sky,
It sounds like a dirty train going past, making a loud noise,
It feels like having a tummy ache,
Sadness is not good, so it gives us a fright!

**Pierce Newton (10)**
**Maylandsea Community Primary School, Chelmsford**

## Happiness

Happiness is the colour red like a beating heart
It tastes like doughnuts with chocolate sprinkles
It smells like warm Galaxy chocolate
It looks like a waterfall coming down
It sounds like Heaven, a beautiful place.

**Tyler Robinson (9)**
**Maylandsea Community Primary School, Chelmsford**

# Happiness

Happiness is the colour of a rainbow,
It tastes like cookies with chocolate chips in them,
It smells like fresh water from a waterfall,
It looks like a waterfall coming down,
It sounds like a waterfall pouring from the top of a mountain,
Happiness feels warm and soft.

**Megan Plumb (9)**
Maylandsea Community Primary School, Chelmsford

# Love

Love is red because it is the colour of your heart,
Love tastes like bubblegum,
Love smells like flowers dancing in the wind,
Love looks like balloons floating up into the blue sky,
Love sounds like a waterfall dripping,
Love feels like my belly doing somersaults.

**Ellie Godley (9)**
**Maylandsea Community Primary School, Chelmsford**

## Love Is Like . . .

A meteorite crashing into a thousand pieces,
Love feels like the first touch of velvet silks soft as the one in Paradise,
It looks like a bolt of lightning flashing before your eyes,
Love taste like a strong, spicy curry, burning through your heart,
It sounds like a storm throwing all of its strength on the top
                              of the whole universe!
Love smells like a cold, damp forest with no life,
Love feels like a bolt of lightning through your heart,
It tastes like the strongest thing that ever walked the Earth,
It sounds like the wind coming at you at 100 miles per hour,
Feels like a range of lightning going through your heart,
A fire coming up into your life burning you to ashes.

**Talia Karim (10)**
**Morton CE Primary School, Bourne**

## The Worst Feelings

Anger sounds like a glass smashing,
Fear sounds like the screams of people in a prison cell,
Anger feels like the Devil taking over you,
Fear feels like a person stalking you in the night.

And it tastes like something sickly in your mouth,
Fear smells like blood on the ground,
Fear looks like the darkness outside at night.

Anger looks like the sight of your parents dying.

**Ryan Compton (9)**
**Morton CE Primary School, Bourne**

# Fun

Fun is your fluffy teddy at bedtime.
It is fireworks on a cold autumn night; it is the stale oil
                                                on a roller coaster,
And also some roasted marshmallows on a cold winter's night.

Fun is the shouts of children as they play a game.
It is the feeling of bouncing on a bouncy castle,
It is a giant smiley face that wants to love you
It is the fresh air; you inhale as you play a game outside.

Fun is your home-made birthday cake,
Fun is your child.

**Edward Mumby (10)**
Morton CE Primary School, Bourne

# Darkness

Feels like a wicked witch.
Casting spells upon me.

Darkness sounds like thunder crashing over my world,
Darkness tastes like the poison entering my mouth,
Darkness looks like the street lamps flickering in the distance,
Darkness smells like the dew in the morning,
Darkness feels like pain in my heart,
Darkness smells like earth, straight after the rain.

Darkness sounds like sinister footsteps of something creeping up
behind you . . .

**Renee Dams (9)**
**Morton CE Primary School, Bourne**

# Sadness

Sadness is silence,
Sadness looks like despair overcoming one's life,
Sadness looks like a river of smiles turning into a sea of tears.

Sadness smells like fresh blood from a hunter's dog's captive,
Sadness smells like wet, damp moss on an eerie night.

Sadness sounds like someone crying in pain and grief,
Sadness sounds like a wolf howling after being awakened from
                                                           his long winter sleep.

Sadness feels like the life seeping into a pit of loneliness,
Sadness feels like you're the last person on Earth.

Sadness taste like the last tear,
Sadness taste like a freshly picked lemon in your mouth.

Sadness . . . gives me tears.

**Georgia Thirtle (9)**
**Morton CE Primary School, Bourne**

## Differences Between Anger And Love

Anger feels like
Fire burning down my spine,
Love feels like
Peace to the world.

Anger sounds like
A volcano about to erupt,
Love sounds like
A boat sailing on the peaceful sea.

Anger smells like the
Blood of a human being.
Love smells like
Flowers in the colourful garden.

Anger tastes like
Gunpowder, hitting my tongue,
Love tastes like
A gift from God.

Anger looks like
Asteroids bursting through the planet,
Love looks like
A dove flying high above.

Anger and love.

**Lewis Pressley (11)**
Morton CE Primary School, Bourne

## Senses And Emotions

Anger feels like steam burning out of my ears,
Anger looks like two men brawling in a pub!
Anger taste like a bitter lemon from off the floor,
Anger smells like the ash of my burnt down house.

Light feels like being a great vulture soaring through the air,
Light sounds like a harp playing sweetly.
Light looks like Almighty God, descending from Heaven,
Light tastes like a luxurious roast dinner warming my mouth.

Silence looks like a choir, just not singing,
Silence feels like a new pair of fluffy slippers.
Silence taste like food after a lost battle,
Silence sounds like, well, nothing . . .

**Jack Smith (10)**
Morton CE Primary School, Bourne

# Anger

Anger smells like a man who has been dead
For a thousand years, and a man being burned alive.

And it tastes like a scuffle gone pop,
Some rotten apple being shoved down your throat.

Anger sounds like Satan laughing at someone's cry,
A woman screaming, but no one to hear her.

Anger feels like a gravestone frozen solid,
A man having his heart broken in two . . .

Anger looks like a man getting vengeance.
With his bare hands . . .

**Alastair Pope (10)**
Morton CE Primary School, Bournea

# The Fear Of My Life!

Fear feels like a hungry wolf, ready to rip you to shreds,
Fear feels like a haunted house in front of me.
And trees and thorn bushes surrounding me,
Fear feels like sharp claws running along my soft skin.
Fear feels like dark magic spreading horrible diseases,
Fear feels like a poisonous spider growing and growing and growing,
Fear feels like an electric bolt hitting me.

Fear sounds like an everlasting scream in my head,
Fear sounds like doors slamming around me,
Fear sounds like a trembling volcano about to explode.
Fear sounds like an echoing voice of the spirit in my heart,
Fear sounds like someone shouting harshly at my friend,
Fear sounds like heavy footsteps getting louder and louder and getting closer and closer.

Ahhh . . .

**Hannah Thompson (9)**
Morton CE Primary School, Bourne

## Love

Love smells like strawberry cake
Being cooked in the oven
On a still summer's night.

Love looks like
A white graceful swan floating in the water
On a bright summer's afternoon.

Love tastes like
Chocolate cream
Melting in your mouth on a winter's day.

Love feels like
Sitting next to the fire
And your heart tingling inside.

Love sounds like
Birds singing and
Wolves howling for their cubs.

That's what love is!

**Kayleigh Lambe (9)**
**Morton CE Primary School**

## Love Is Like . . .

Love looks like a dove sailing through the air.
Love feels like your heart splitting into two.
Love taste like a hot chocolate with marshmallows on top.
Love sounds like the calm ocean.
Love smells like the fresh morning air in the summer.
Love looks like someone madly in love.
Love taste like some sour wine running down someone's throat.
Love smells like a roast turkey dinner.
Love sounds like someone singing, a lovely melody.
Love feels like someone getting a divorce after a big fight.

**Shannon McPherson (10)**
**Morton CE Primary School, Bourne**

# What Is Sadness?

Sadness is a mean thought,
But sometimes it is nice.

Sadness looks like a river of tears,
Flooding the cities and towns,
Hurting and killing people.

It sounds like the shouting of people
Wanting help to save lives,
After a shocking tsunami.

It tastes like the dying man's last supper,
With his family and friends.

It smells like the flavour of the burning candle,
With wax dripping down.

It feels like a shiver down your spine.
When a relative has died.

**Jack Graham (10)**
**Morton CE Primary School, Bourne**

# Darkness

Darkness makes me scared.

Darkness feels like the Earth going into an eclipse and never coming out.
Darkness smells like the body of a dead animal rotting away.
Darkness tastes like people dying.
Darkness looks like a pitch-black tunnel that never ends.
Darkness sounds like a wolf howling at the stroke of midnight.

Darkness feels like a black bubble around the Earth blocking all light.
Darkness smells like a little girl in a burning house with no escape.
Darkness tastes like a rotten apple, drenched in blood.
Darkness looks like a black hole that destroys everything in sight.

*Darkness sounds like . . .*

**Craig Turner (10)**
Morton CE Primary School, Bourne

## Laughter And Happiness

The TV is broken and Mum is getting angry.
The children come in and they're getting hungry.
The noise is getting worse until Mum shouts, 'Pipe down, shut up.'

The next day the children go off to school,
They're late for class, so they run through the hall.
The teacher catches them and sends them to class.
Their mum finds out and sends them to bed.
And they wonder, *what is fun? What is happiness?*
And they decide . . .

Happiness tastes like a gorgeous Sunday lunch right in front of you.
Happiness feels like all your friends are caring for you.
Happiness looks like friends all playing together.
Happiness smells like candyfloss at the fairground.
Happiness sounds like children that are laughing in the distance.
And think maybe, life is not so bad after all!

**Ashley Dacre (10)**
**Morton CE Primary School, Bourne**

## Silence And Fear

Silence looks like the misty moon appearing for the first time,
Silence feels like the stroke of midnight.
Silence feels like a predator that has found its prey.
And silence looks like a massive destruction that has shattered
                                                                      the Earth.
Silence smells there's a sense of death in the air
And silence is . . .

Fear tastes like sheer bitterness, sipped out of a ghostly cup.
This sounds like a glass smashing against the wall.
The fear feels like the floor shaking underfoot.
Fear looks like a feather pen writing on its own.
And fear looks like a boy's face turning pale after a dreadful nightmare.

**Liam Davidson (10)**
Morton CE Primary School, Bourne

## Laughter

What is laughter?

Laughter looks like a newborn baby, playing on your bed.
Laughter smells like the new compost in with the pansies.
Laughter tastes like a rich chocolate birthday cake, melting
 in your mouth.
Laughter sounds like the sweet call of a little dolphin.
Laughter feels like your old, ripped-out teddy bear, you cuddle in bed.

That's what laughter is!

**Talys Andres (9)**
**Morton CE Primary School, Bourne**

# Senses

Hate looks like a million hearts breaking,
Hate feels like a burst of killing rushing through your body,
Hate smells like rotten blood from the never-ending murders,
Hate tastes like a dreadful battle inside you,
Hate sounds like the wail of a visitor to Heaven.

Love looks like a wonderful gift from God,
Love feels like the softness of home,
Love smells like a soft fragrance in the air,
Love taste like some glorious amber nectar,
Love sounds like an angel playing a harp.

Light looks like the gateway to Heaven,
Light feels like an amazing warmth surrounding you,
Light smells like a love message from God,
Light taste like a million gifts,
Light is a gift from God.

**Davin Phenix (10)**
Morton CE Primary School, Bourne

# A Pocketful of Poetry

Anger smells like a volcano ready to erupt.
And it tastes like red hot chilli peppers burning in your mouth.
Anger feels like a fist splitting your heart in half.
Anger looks like someone going red, fit to burst.
Anger sounds like a stampede, getting louder and louder.

Happiness smells like a fresh bunch of roses.
Happiness, sounds like a family laughing, joyfully together.
Happiness looks like a couple getting married.
Happiness taste like sweet icing sugar, melting on your tongue.
Happiness feels like the warmth of a fire burning.

**Felicity Mitchell (9)**
**Morton CE Primary School, Bourne**

# Feelings

Sadness looks like a dying deer by the side of the road
on a cold winter's day.
Sadness sounds like the rain pattering on the window sill
in a wild storm.
Sadness smells like the last leaf of autumn,
drifting to the woodland floor.
Sadness taste like salty tears dropping from a face.
Sadness feels like cloth, fading into grey.

Hate is the crack of a hunter's whip in a dark forest.
Hate tastes like sour lemon juice, trickling down your throat.
Hate feels like a cruel library of cold stone on your face.
Hate looks like the hunt ending with the final bang!
Hate smells like fresh blood in the morning.

**Jennifer McAndrew (9)**
Morton CE Primary School, Bourne

# Love

Love beautiful love.

Love looks like newborn rabbits hopping in the meadows.
Love feels like watching the robin fly in the winter moonlight.
Love tastes like the most indulgent chocolate that melts in your mouth.
Love smells like the most perfectly bloomed petunia.
Love sounds like music at a classical theatre.

Love looks like two doves resting in a wooden nest.
Love feels like remembering the first time you stepped into the sea.
Love tastes like watermelon that runs down your throat
                                          like a meandering river.
Love smells like fresh dew on the autumn grass.
Love sounds like the birds singing on a Sunday afternoon.

Love is me.

**Georgina Wilkie (10)**
Morton CE Primary School, Bourne

## Love

Love looks like a rainbow
Appearing in the crystal-blue sky.

Love sounds like the birds
Singing in the morning.

Love smells like the reddest
Of all roses.

Love feels like a soft pillow
That you snuggle into.

Love tastes like a melting chocolate
In your mouth.

**Eleanor Davies (10)**
Morton CE Primary School, Bourne

# Anger

Anger is like a hurricane ripping through the night sky.
Anger looks like an eruption from a volcano.

Anger looks like fireworks on a frosty night.
Anger makes me feel lonely.

Anger tastes like poison on the tip of my tongue.
Anger smells like a raging fire, out of control.

**Callum Lusty (11)**
**Morton CE Primary School, Bourne**

# What Is Anger?

Anger is a bomb breaking the world!
It feels like an axe chopping through your life.
It feels that your heart is crashing through a pounding wall.
And it tastes like the last sip of blood trickling down your mouth.
It smells of burning wood running up your nose.
It smells of fuzzy old sock ripped up in a bin.
It sounds like rain thundering on a windowpane.
It looks like a glass smashing through a door.
It looks like thunder crashing through a house.

Anger makes me sick!

**Samuel Doe (10)**
Morton CE Primary School, Bourne

## Both Sides Of The Story

Happiness sounds like the children laughing in the meadow.
Happiness feels like the love from your own family.
Happiness looks like the smiles on all the people's faces.
Happiness tastes like the most delicious meal, you have ever had.
Happiness smells like a beautiful field of roses.

Sadness tastes like the dead bodies, you have to eat to stay alive.
Sadness smells like the perfume of your dead grandma.
Sadness sounds like a teardrop hitting the hard ground.
Sadness feels like the loneliness of the whole world.
Sadness looks like someone in your family dying.

**James Thomas (10)**
**Morton CE Primary School, Bourne**

## The Five Senses Of Fear

Fear feels like the goosebumps on your arm,
Fear sounds like a scream in a dark misty wood with no one around
to hear.

Fear looks like a corpse in a dark cemetery,
Fear tastes like the horrible blood from a human,
Fear smells like the air in a dark forest.

Fear feels like a cold bloody hand,
Fear sounds like the Twin Towers falling to the ground,
Fear looks like a wounded lamb,
Fear tastes like a thousand-year-old bottle of wine,
Fear smells like a dead body . . .

**Michael Montgomery (9)**
Morton CE Primary School, Bourne

# Peace

Peace is dolphins
Swimming in the
Water, leaping.
Over the waves.

It is relaxation
Watching the sun,
Go down, seagulls
Flying over your head.

Peace is a flower
Budding in the spring.
Making lots of pretty
Colours, for you and me to see.

It is sleeping.
When the winter.
Comes, wake up bright
And early when the snowfalls.

**Megan Slinger (9)**
Rampton Primary, Retford

# Peace

Peace is a dove
As white as snow
Flying the air.
Like a cloud in the sky.

It is love
In the air.
Like a dolphin
Splashing in the water.

Peace is a tree.
Blowing me in the wind.
With birds relaxing
In the big green tree.

It is as quiet.
As the wind.
With the bird.
Singing in the tree.

It is a pet dog.
Sleeping in its bed.
As calm
As a dove.

**James Lofthouse (10)**
**Rampton Primary, Retford**

## Peace

Peace is a dolphin
Splashing around
In the soft warm sea
Of the Caribbean seas.

It is relaxation
Running through your blood.
Comfy, squidgy feeling
Of comfort.

Peace is a flower
Swaying in the
East wind in the
Meadow of grass.

It is Love
All around you.
Hugging you.
All day long.

**Scarlett Cordall (9)**
**Rampton Primary, Retford**

# Peace

Peace is a dove
White-headed
In the blowing wind
Of New York

It is a dolphin
Swimming in the sea
Playing in the sea
Around Cornwall.

Peace is care.
Soft and somehow
Quiet every way.
Sailing on sea.

It is quiet land
Where we sleep in peace.
Nowhere noisy.
On the bed, quiet.

**Hayden Birkett (9)**
**Rampton Primary, Retford**

# Peace

Peace is a chicken
All brown-feathered
Laying an egg
In the mountain-cold snow.

It is a pencil.
All bright colours
Doing nothing all day
Apart from colouring in.

Peace is a quiet room
Lots of fresh air
But no one to enjoy it
Other than a bright blue ladybug.

It is a cheesy garden gnome
Eating all the cheese
Living a joyful life
Playing in the cheese.

Peace is the end of war
No more fighting
No more killing
All making friends.

Peace is caramel
All slushy and creamy
Being eaten by whales
Beside the sea

**Josh Gillott (11) & Jack Eddy (10)**
Rampton Primary, Retford

## Peace

Peace is the sky
Blue is the sea.
Peace can be a dolphin
Doing the Mexican wave
Peace can be relaxation.
Sleeping all day.
It is a promise
To keep your love
And hug all the time.
Peace is a petal
Blown by the drifting clouds.
It is silence at the beach
At noon watching the sea go by.

**Carter Marson (9)**
**Rampton Primary, Retford**

# Peace

Peace is a dove,
Flying over Heaven,
As graceful as a swan,
Gliding over rainbows.

It is dolphins,
Underwater,
Swimming through the sea,
Trying to catch fish as big as they could.

Peace is a caterpillar,
Crawling through the sky,
Watching the stars go by,
Stretching left and right.

It is the sun,
Shining day and night,
Watching the moon pass through the night sky,
Trying to catch a flight.

**Lucy Presley (9)**
**Rampton Primary, Retford**

# Dying

I'm lying in the trench,
It's as hot as a heatwave,
Golden bullets are strewn on the floor,
One of them in my arm,
Bodies lying twisted and mangled on the floor,
People falling back on barbed wire,
Bangs and crashes,
People's feet splattered in mud.

I'm lying in the trench,
Excruciating pain running through my body,
I might not be alive tomorrow,
The shelters remind me of the attic at home,
Lord of Lords, help me through this pain
I would do anything to make it stop,
Finally, a medic has sorted out my arm,
I'm back on my feet, I fire my Tommy gun.

And again, I'm lying in the trench.

**Nicholas Kemp (10)**
St Peter's Primary School, Colchester

# Dying

I'm lying in the trench
Staring at the stiff bodies of my fallen comrades on the floor.
Bullets are streaming over my head.
I feel like I am at Death's door.

I am lying in the trench.
Feeling like I'm dead
I've lost the feeling in my knee.
And at the food the rats begin to gnaw.
My commanding officer tells me, 'Get up and fire,'
I stay staring at the ring I wear
Reminds me of the one on my wife's fair finger
I remember my job from which only a week ago, I retired.
I force myself in this life to linger.

I am lying in the trench
The Hun is getting closer
We have lost, I fear.
The officer orders me again and I reply, 'No sir,'
A comrade says, he has longed for the taste of beer
Then he entered eternal sleep.

But I'm still lying in the trench.

**George Styles (10)**
**St Peter's Primary School, Colchester**

## Dying

I'm lying in a trench
Waiting for the signal to fire.
Explosions are as loud as fireworks
I pray to God to help me survive this war
Rats are eating our supplies.
I tell those despicable Germans,
'Go to Hell and never return'.

**Oliver Dean (10)**
St Peter's Primary School, Colchester

# Dying

I am lying in the trench
Stiffs and rats all around me.
And the officer shouting,
'Get up! Get up!'
We need many men,
To me it was a human slaughterhouse
I'm feeling like a scared hen.
With bullets flying near me.
And then I had to say.
I wish I could return to Blighty
God bless these men
Will I live?

I am lying in the trench.
I can hear children's voices.
Flying round my head.
And then they say.
Stop this horrific manslaughter
I wish there was total peace
And then a bomb goes off . . .
I am so scared
Besides, I am only 18 . . .

**Thomas Randerson (10)**
St Peter's Primary School, Colchester

# Dying

I am lying in the trench.
It's like a suicidal booth.
Will I become a stiff?
I'll soon find out the truth.

I am lying in the trench.
There's a bullet in my arm, shiny and long.
I'll hopefully get back to Blighty.
And go back where I belong.

**Angus Unsworth (11)**
St Peter's Primary School, Colchester

# Dying

I'm lying in the trench.
Cockroaches like bullets
Skimming the ground.

I'm lying in the trench
A golden bullet skinned my ear
Reminding me of my daughter's golden hair.

I'm lying in the trench
Praying to God that I'll survive this putrid war.

I'm lying in the trench.
Trying to survive.

**Luke Norman (10)**
St Peter's Primary School, Colchester

# Dying

I'm lying in a trench
There are no short cuts
It is not smooth like Heaven.
It is all bumpy like Hell.

The provisions are horrible.
Corned beef tastes like maggots
I'm not seeing Blighty
I'm seeing hell.

Stiffs all around me
Absorbing every conversation I've ever had.
Wooden props remind me of home.
This mob is clenching my throat.
I feel children's voices in my head.
Cheering for their dad.

This war makes me want to stand up to the Germans and say,
'Take me cruel world'.
This world was peaceful.
Until someone crosses the line.

**William Mills (11)**
**St Peter's Primary School, Colchester**

# Dying

I am lying in the trench,
With brass bullets flying all around me,
Like harmless little stones,
Waiting for something to happen.

I am lying in the trench,
My body cold and heavy
Alex is by my side,
Pleading with me not to go.

I am lying in the trench,
With mud in my hair and rats at my legs,
The Hun is getting closer, defeating all our troops,
I can hear them overhead.

I am lying in the trench,
Oh Lord,
Please help me,
I beg of you,
I am weak, I am helpless.

I am lying in the trench,
I am ill with the lack of food,
The bullet in my arm feels like fire,
Creeping slowly along my body.

I'm lying in a trench,
Alex has found my letter that my wife wrote to me,
It reminds me of home.
And how I longed to be there.

I am lying in the trench,
Please help me Lord,
I am dying.

**Charlotte Self (10)**
St Peter's Primary School, Colchester

## Lying And Dying In The Trench

I am lying in the trench,
People are being shot to pieces,
The air is as cold as the North Pole,
People are shooting gold bullets.
That looked like a jaguar's teeth,
The mud is filled with rats and worms
The blood is flowing like red wine,
Oh God, please help me,
Please stop this war.

**Joshua Forbes-Brown (10)**
St Peter's Primary School, Colchester

## Dying In The Trench

I am lying in the trench.
Dying, dying, dying,
Golden bullet shells, remind me of my wife's hair clips.
Rats all around me, biting me.

I am lying in the trench
My hands and feet numb as can be.
Oh Lord to die is a shame!
Until then, I wish oh Lord to go back to England.
Oh Lord, stop this dreadful war.
Let us return to our homeland of England,
Ireland, Scotland and Wales, and many other lands.

Oh Lord, stop this war,
Stop hatred.
Stop the deaths.
Make tranquillity.

Oh Lord, this is my final prayer.
For I am dying.

**Aaron Osborne (10)**
St Peter's Primary School, Colchester

## Move Him Into The Sun

Move him in into the sun.
And perhaps he'll remember
The first morning
He awoke in Madrid
With the sun shining through
The transparent windows.

Move him into the fog
And perhaps he'll remember
The steam appearing through
The shower curtain.

Move him into the rain
And perhaps he'll remember
The ocean at Brightlingsea
When the cool waves
Splashed over his forehead.

Move him into the wind
And perhaps he'll remember.
The breeze rushing past his face
When he took his dog Jimmy
On his first ever walk.

So move him into any of these
And perhaps he'll remember life.

**Jack O'Byrne (10)**
St Peter's Primary School, Colchester

# Sea

Here I go out to sea.
To find my clothes that got washed away from me
The big wave as big as a block of flats
Brought my clothes back to me.

**Ellie Newton (9)**
**Thanet Primary School, Hull**

## The Sea

As soft as the breeze!
But sometimes as dangerous as a fire!
The safe soothing sea.
The dangerous, daring sea.

**Sophie-Claire Webster (9)**
Thanet Primary School, Hull

## Waterfall

Waterfalls are like standing under the world's biggest shower,
Waterfalls look so beautiful, all the clear water,
Zooming down very quickly,
*Splish, splash.*

**Jade Wiles (9)**
Thanet Primary School, Hull

# The Battle For Britannia

On the eve of battle,
Dare I say,
Constantly rattle
And then pray
This battle,
Stomach churning as Emperor Claudius' sword
Swiping a soldier.

Worried that I will be left dead,
Or lucky alive,
To be a Roman, takes courage,
Sturdiness, stamina, strength.
Confused as a lost dog,
Wondering how to get home.

Trusty armour to defend my honour,
Campfires ablaze,
Warriors ablaze thinking hard,
How to beat the Britons.
For now,
We must get that energy to rise, in order to obtain Britannia.

**Luke Eeles (10)**
**Waddington Redwood Primary School, Lincoln**

# The Wind

It makes me feel cheerful,
The wind is like a mother soothing me.
The wind makes me crazy,
It fills me with joy.

On windy mornings, it makes me run with delight.
Sometimes it makes me angry,
When it pulls my clothes away.
It makes me feel like I'm flying.

**Molly Barker (9)**
**Waddington Redwood Primary School, Lincoln**

## The Wind

The whistling wind gives you a freezing feeling,
and you shiver until you're dead frozen.
The wind makes me feel annoyed when it pulls you,
in every direction.
It's weird when you get pushed back,
like a bulldozer forcing you back in time.

Swirling wind is very dangerous when chucking things
everywhere, it's like a game of dodgeball,
but instead it's for your life.

I hear the wind coming straight towards me,
smashing against my face.

**John Melligan (10)**
Waddington Redwood Primary School, Lincoln

# The Wind

Mighty wind, pounding me like a tornado coming right at me.
As loud as a power station making electricity.
It just makes me feel mad,
Sometimes I want to punch someone.
But I just get on with life like a normal person.
So when the wind comes, I just do what I would normally do.

**Lewis Anthony (9)**
Waddington Redwood Primary School, Lincoln

# The Wind

The blustery wind, the boisterous wind,
Pushes me back, trying to escape, trembling.
Close and near, the turbulent wind,
Unbreakable and invincible.
Windows smashed,
Cars crashed.
Running, running away, far away.

Trees destroyed, plants crushed,
Clouds above slowly drifting.
Up the hill, the very high hill,
I see the houses, the windows, the cars.
I hear the wind as it whistles behind me,
Thinking, thinking of why the wind is here.

**Caitlin Barker (10)**
Waddington Redwood Primary School, Lincoln

## The Battle For Britannia
Thought ricocheting it through my inquisitive mind,
Worrying, will I still be here?
As I stare up to the milky moon, I pray for my family.
Loud noises of people talking.
Somebody tapped on my cold muscly shoulder,
I was dreaming though,
About how tomorrow would be!

**Lauren Burnley (10)**
**Waddington Redwood Primary School, Lincoln**

## Invasion Of Britannia

The sea is an angry lion, frustrated and annoyed.
The thunder is an angry bear, with a deep stare.
The lightning is a vicious grey snake,
I'm feeling nervous and lonely but ready to go.

I'm sat here all alone, preparing for the battle.
Grooming my special horse, polishing my mighty armour.
I'm shivering and shaking, I feel so unknown.

I'm in my position now. Ready to fight.
I know I can do it using my Roman might.
The Celts, they are a whirlwind charging at us,
My sword cuts through legs and arms, there is blood everywhere,
It's a horrible thing we do, but we don't have to care.

The smell of dead bodies is horrible.
I nearly did die; I'm feeling so sad.
The fight was a furious stampeding rhino.
It will be a long time now until I'm home.

**Charlotte Flint (10)**
Waddington Redwood Primary School, Lincoln

# Roman Invasion

The sea is a stampeding elephant, running this way and that.
The lightning is fireworks exploding in the sky.
The boat is a see-saw rocking to and fro.
I feel scared and frightened, I know I'm going to die.

I'm sat here all alone, preparing for the battle.
Grooming my special horse, polishing all my armour.
The Celts won't stand a chance against our power.
The battle draws ever closer, hour by hour.

After three the charge, one, two, three!
The Celts looked rather fierce staring down at us.
My friend's already gone, an arrow in his eye.
But in the end we won again, victory is mine.

Arms and legs everywhere, bodies even too.
Yes, the Celts are dead, now the world is ours.
I can't wait to see my wife and children.
Shedding all my tears, for my mighty friends.

**Hayley Flint (10)**
**Waddington Redwood Primary School, Lincoln**

# Roman Invasion

The sea is an angry lion, looking for its prey.
The boat is a big see-saw, throwing itself away.
The clouds are big elephants, big, dark and grey.
Here I am, looking so brave, on this big boat faraway.
I'm sat here all alone, preparing for tomorrow.
Grooming my special horse, polishing my mighty armour.
The Celts won't stand a chance against a mighty power,
The battle draws closer, hour by agonising hour.

All of my preparations are ready now, for the fierce battle.
We all met at the battlefield, on that cold day.
Then the battle began, I made the first shot.
Then they darted their arrows, and hit my friend a lot.

Dead and dying all around, the Celts, they are defeated.
The Roman army has survived, the Empire is completed.
We have to stay around, although we do not want to.

Home is so far, far away, it's just something I had to do.

**Gezamin Parry**
Waddington Redwood Primary School, Lincoln

# Invasion Of Britannia

The wind is a windy dragon, trying to freeze my face.
The rain is like elephants stampeding across the desert.
The waves are a bear roaring.
I'm not scared, we are Romans, and I am not scared,
I am excited.

I'm sat here all alone, preparing for tomorrow,
Grooming my special horse, polishing my mighty armour.
The Celts won't stand a chance against our power.
The battle draws ever closer, hour by hour.

I am nowhere near scared, so far we're winning.
I know they're very weak, I know they are savages,
I know I'm very strong, and I am going to win.
I know I'm very strong, and we are sure to win.

I have been winded, and my foot has been chopped off,
And I end the battle in pain.
I am near death, home so far away, I wish that I was there.
But I am here in Britain, a cold and lonely place.

**Carys Thomas**
Waddington Redwood Primary School, Lincoln

# Roman Invasion

The boat was like a suit of armour, protecting against the seas,
The sea was like an angry bull, trying to charge at me,
The sky was like a black cave, hanging up above,
I feel scared, like I might not survive, missing my family's love.

I'm sat here worrying about tomorrow, it's drawing ever near,
The battle is going to be furious, and I will show no fear.
I'm making my sword so sharp, it will cut through arms and legs,
I can see my family in the fire, looking over me.

I can see the Celts now, they look very fierce,
I take my sword from my side and charge, full with lots of fear.
I'm fighting as hard as I can, all strong and fierce,
The Celts' hearts are ours.

We finally won the battle, I'm cheering with all my might,
I've lost a lot of men, but don't worry, we'll burn them tonight.
I'm going all the way back home to see my wife and child,
I'm waiting to see them today, with joy in my heart.

**James Ekins**
Waddington Redwood Primary School, Lincoln

## The Battle For Britannia
Rivers of troubled thoughts gushed through my mind,
Still and silent.
Questions racing around in my head,
Will I live, or will I die?

Determined, like a vicious lion,
Searching for his prey,
Sharpening my shining sword ready for victory,
Preparing my mind, so my life carries on!

Sitting at the bright, burning campfire,
Loud noises,
Cold breeze,
Green glowing eyes,
Staring at me.
My shield, sword, armour, will it protect me?
Will I win, or will I lose?

**Emily Pavier (10)**
**Waddington Redwood Primary School, Lincoln**

# The Wind

The raging wind is an angry dog
With jagged teeth ready to skin me
And take me away.

The wind is a wild horse freely running
Through the meadow with the wind
Through her hair.

The wind is a howling wolf.
On the top of the cliff eating
His awful prey.

The wind is like a speedboat
Speeding through the water
As fast as the fastest car on Earth.

The wind is like an eagle
Soaring high above the mountains
Watching for his next kill.

The wind is like a jet fighter plane.
Zooming through the skies
Faster than a lightning bolt.

**Sara Edwards**
**Waddington Redwood Primary School, Lincoln**

# The Wind

Brushing through the trees, the wind,
A golden eagle,
Swoops down,
Attacking helpless prey.

Breeze is like a gentle butterfly,
Fluttering into
Ominous mist,
Freely, not knowing where to go next.

Tender, soothing, gale,
Wing-like.
Supporting cruising crows,
With slow, gentle movement.

Almighty wind,
Rough as bark,
Says, 'I am wild, I am great,
I travel, strong, powerful, crazy and straight'.

Mighty, lean.
The wind is great,
An enraged rhino
With his mate.

He might not survive,
His friend might,
But only if they don't
Have a fight.

**Jay Bellis (9)**
**Waddington Redwood Primary School, Lincoln**

# The Battle Of Britannia

The eve of the battle,
Is making my heart cold as ice,
My sharp sword,
My glistening armour,
I am prepared to go,
I am determined to begin,
I pray each night,
For everything, I think of.

We are going to Britannia,
It is frightening for some,
They defeated us before,
We are strong enough,
Vicious enough,
My knees are shaking,
There is wind going through me.

A while until the battle,
Being trained,
Sharpening my sword,
Anything to make myself vicious,
Clanging, crashing,
The noises from our camp,
Striking of heads,
Will it be mine?

**Aimee Hayward (10)**
Waddington Redwood Primary School, Lincoln

# Roman Soldier

The sea was an angry giant, waving a blanket.
The rain was like icicles, falling on my head.
The clouds are as black as the Black Knight's armour.
I feel prepared and brave for battle.

I'm sat here worrying about tomorrow, it's drawing ever near,
The battle will be furious, and I will show no fear.
I'm sharpening my shiny swords,
Tomorrow, they will be covered in blood.

Today is the day we fight,
The Celts will get a fright.
Now the Celts are charging,
And I am feeling fierce.

I have lost an arm and leg,
And do not feel calm.
I'm glad I have survived,
I'm proud I'm still alive.

**Jack Woolsey (10)**
**Waddington Redwood Primary School, Lincoln**

# Roman Soldier

The sea was an angry dog, beating a million drums.
The wind was a strong rhino, trying to blow me over.
The rain cloud was a firework ready to explode.
Here I sit, trying to put on a brave face.

I'm sat here all alone, preparing for tomorrow.
Grooming my lovely horse, polishing my mighty armour.
The Celts won't stand a chance against our power,
The battle draws closer, hour by agonising hour.

We walked through the long fens, me and my men.
There we see the Celts, so we draw our swords.
I tell my men to charge, just to think that we are going to win.
We have Britannia and the Celts were so proud.

I only escaped with a few of my men, but my mate's leg was gone,
I took my army back to camp,
Next day, we sailed back to Rome,
Claudius came out to meet us with all the people too.

**Kelly Warren (10)**
Waddington Redwood Primary School, Lincoln

# Roman Invasion

The sea is a mad dog barking at the moon,
The wind is a stampeding horse running away,
The boat is a rattlesnake chasing after its prey,
Me and my crew are crushed mice in the hold.

I'm sat here preparing for the battle tomorrow,
While I discuss my army's tactics, lions stalking at night,
Polishing my armour, ready for the fight,
We blow out the fire and rest for the big day.

It was the dawn of the big day today,
I swing my sword, from left to right,
Someone cut my hand; like a bear's claw slicing,
But bravely I ride on to defeat my enemy.

After the battle we were victorious,
The pain was like a blazing fire, shooting through my arm,
We returned to camp, but never returned to the battleground,
We lost lots of brave men that night, and they were never found.

**Robbie Green (10)**
**Waddington Redwood Primary School, Lincoln**

## The Crushing Of The Celts

The sea was a furious lion fighting for survival,
The boat is a tiny insect floating on the waves,
The thunder is a fire-breathing dragon roaring in my ear,
I'm feeling scared and frightened, I think I'm going to die.

I'm sat here all alone, preparing for tomorrow,
Grooming my special horse, polishing my mighty armour,
Got my tactics ready, 'Come on, Britain, we are ready'.
I see the Celts in my head, I'm not scared of them.

They are there, on the top of the hill, the Celts have arrived,
I'm talking to my wife now, whilst I'm still alive.
Arms off, legs off, blood everywhere,
Horses down, people down, smell of the rotten dead,
But in the end, we won again and victory is mine.

We're at camp now, eating food, thinking in my head,
I can't wait to see our family,
And yes, the Celts are dead!

**Jake Rigby (10)**
Waddington Redwood Primary School, Lincoln